A 3-minute forever book

EAT YOUR PEAS®

※ for Tough Times

By Cheryl Karpen
Gently Spoken

2014

Melissa

For My beautiful daughter
Love From _____ Mom _____

Blessings always
honey!

At the heart of this
little book
is a **promise**.

It's a promise from
me to you
and it goes like this:

If you ever need someone to talk to
(really talk to),
someone to hear
(really hear),
what's on your mind and in your heart,
call me.

Call me early. Call me late.
Just call me.

I promise
to listen to you
with all my
heart,
with all my
attention,
and without
interrupting.

What's more,
I promise to cherish you,
to lift you up
and (if I can help it)
never, ever let you down.

In the meantime,
here are a
few things
I'd like you
to know,
remember,
and
never, ever doubt.

No matter what
challenges come your way,
always remember
you are loved.

Truly loved.

It takes courage to
get through
tough times.

You can do it.

I believe in you.

Some days,
getting out of bed
is an act of
bravery.

Those are the days
you are
my hero.

Remember the first tender colors of green when trees come to life in the spring?

Or the marvel that tired old caterpillars turn into flamboyant butterflies?

Be on the lookout for reminders of *hope*.

They're everywhere.

Each new sunrise
is a
reminder
that every day
is a
new
beginning.

I'm keeping you close in my heart and near in my prayers.

Having faith
means it isn't necessary
to have all of
the answers.

I can't promise everything will be okay.

But I can promise to do everything in my power to make it better.

No wonder
Let Go and Let God
has given so many
the courage
to face another day.

Tears
are
raindrops
of
hope.

Everyday
celebrate yourself
for who you are.

A kind,
wonderful
and
cherished
individual.

Treat yourself like you would your own best friend.

Talk to yourself with *love*, *praise* and encouragement.

Keep your
dreams
and
desires
alive.

*You
are
worthy
of
happiness.*

Look for hope
in the lives
of others.
Listen to their stories
and learn
how they have
made it through
challenging
times.

Be tender
with your heart.

Congratulate yourself
on making it through
another day.

Give yourself a hug.

Spend time doing
something **you love**.

Blessed are
the little joys in life.

They have the power
to keep us going when
we don't think we can.

The surest way through
tough times
is to believe in the power of
one step at a time.

One day farther along.
One more phone call
to someone who cares
deeply about you.

May we always know
how to make each other
smile
and give each other
reason to hope.

Every time
you pick up this little book,
consider yourself
hugged.
And cherished too.

There is no challenge in life so big we can't handle it together.

Remember my promise.

I want to be there for you.

To celebrate
your courage,

to champion
your *dreams*,

and of course,
to remind you to ...

always

eat your peas.

Why Peas?

She was a vibrant, dazzling young woman with a promising future.
Yet, at sixteen, her world felt sad and hopeless.

I was living over 1800 miles away and wanted to let this very special young person in my life know I would be there for her across the miles and through the darkness. I wanted her to know she could call me any time, at any hour, and I would be there for her. And I wanted to give her a piece of my heart she could take with her anywhere—a reminder she was loved.
Really loved.

Her name is Maddy and she was the inspiration for my first PEAS book, **Eat Your Peas for Young Adults**. At the very beginning of her book I made a place to write in my phone number so she knew I was serious about being available. And right beside the phone number I put my promise to listen—*really listen*—whenever that call came.

Soon after the book was published, people began to ask me if I had the same promise and affirmation for adults. I realized it isn't just young people who need to be reminded how truly special they are. We all do.

Today Maddy is thriving and giving hope to others in her life.
If someone has given you this book, it means you are pretty special to them and they wanted to let you know. Take it to heart.

Believe it, and remind yourself often.

Wishing you peas and plenty of joy,

Cheryl Karpen

P.S. My Mama always said, "Eat Your Peas, they're good for you." The pages of this book are filled with nutrients for the heart. They're simply good for you too.

A portion of the profits from the
Eat Your Peas Collection
will benefit empowerment programs
for youth and adults.

With appreciation....

How do you begin to thank all the people who touch
your life—those who make each day better and brighter?
People who exude passion and purpose. People who love doing
what they do and sharing their many gifts.

It is to these individuals, I dedicate this book:
artist, Sandy Fougner; editor, Suzanne Foust; my friend,
Teresa Bechtold; Lana, Kit, Gayle, Stephanie, Barbara, Ray,
Mark and John at Ideal Printers; and my special
cheerleaders, Ramon Hughes and Patricia Coley.

A special thank you to all of the individuals who believe in
the power of PEAS to make a difference in one's life, especially
the little shops who dedicate a place for Eat Your Peas on their
shelves and the readers who call and write to share
their heartfelt stories.

You are my inspiration.

~ CK

If this book has touched your life,
we'd love to hear your story.
Please send it to
mystory@eatyourpeas.com
or mail it to
Gently Spoken
PO Box 245
Anoka, MN 55303

About the author

"Eat Your Peas"

A self-proclaimed dreamer, Cheryl
spends her time imagining and creating
between the historic river town of Anoka, Minnesota
and the seaside village of Islamorada, Florida.

An effervescent speaker, Cheryl brings inspiration,
insight, and humor to corporations,
professional organizations and churches.
Learn more about her at: www.cherylkarpen.com

About the illustrator

Sandy Fougner artfully weaves
a love for design, illustration and
interiors with being a wife
and mother of three sons.

The Eat Your Peas Collection™

is now available in the following titles:

Mothers
Sisters
Sons
Grandkids
Sweethearts
New Moms
Girlfriends

Someone Special
Tough Times
Daughter-in-law
Mother-in-law
Sister-in-law
For the Cure
Extraordinary
 Young Person

New titles are SPROUTING up all the time!

Heart and Soul Collection

To Let You Know I Care
Hope for a Hurting Heart
Can We Try Again? Finding a way back to love

For inspiration and to view a complete collection,
visit us online at **eatyourpeas.com**

Eat Your Peas® for Tough Times

Copyright 2006, Cheryl Karpen
Seventh Printing, July 2012

Homegrown in the USA

For more information or to locate a store near you, contact:

Gently Spoken
PO Box 245
Anoka, MN 55303

Toll-free 1-877-224-7886 or visit us online at
www.eatyourpeas.com

 30% post-consumer recycled paper